Internet DOs & DON'Ts

Don't Share Your Address Online

Shannon Miller

PowerKiDS press

New York

Published in 2014 by The Rosen Publishing Group, Inc.
29 East 21st Street, New York, NY 10010

First Edition

Editor: Jennifer Way
Book Design: Andrew Povolny

Photo Credits: Cover Blend Images/JGI/Jamie Grill/Getty Images; p. 5 Monkey Business/Thinkstock; p. 7 Blend Images/Shutterstock.com; p. 9 Masson/Shutterstock.com; p. 11 iStockphoto/Thinkstock; p. 13 Stockbyte/Thinkstock; p. 15 KidStock/Blend Images; p. 17 Bruce Laurance/The Image Bank/Getty Images; p. 19 Flying Colours Ltd/Digital Vision/Getty Images; p. 21 Yellow Dog Productions/Lifesize/ Getty Images; p. 23 Monkey Business Images/Shutterstock.com.

Library of Congress Cataloging-in-Publication Data

Miller, Shannon.
  Don't share your address online / by Shannon Miller. — First edition.
      pages cm. — (Internet dos & don'ts)
  Includes index.
  ISBN 978-1-4777-1536-9 (library binding) — ISBN 978-1-4777-1558-1 (pbk.) —
  ISBN 978-1-4777-1559-8 (6-pack)
  1. Internet and children—Juvenile literature. 2. Internet users—Juvenile literature. 3. Online etiquette—Juvenile literature. 4. Online sexual predators—Juvenile literature. I. Title.
  HQ784.I58M55 2014
  025.04028'9—dc23
                                        2012050007

Manufactured in the United States of America

CPSIA Compliance Information: Batch #S13PK4: For Further Information contact Rosen Publishing, New York, New York at 1-800-237-9932

Contents

Do you like to go online? There are many fun things on the **Internet**. It is smart to be safe online. This book will tell you how.

Keep facts about yourself **private**. Do not share them online. Your address is a private fact. Never share it online.

A **website** might ask for your address. This tells the website where you live. This could help the website work better. The website may ask for other reasons.

A website can do other things with your address. It can send you **junk mail**. It can sell your address. Then other places can send you junk mail.

Ask an adult to look at the website. He will find out why it wants your address. There may be ways not to share your address.

13

An adult also can find safe websites. They will not ask for your address. Many of them are just for kids.

A stranger might ask for your address online. Do not share your address with strangers! This is very important for your safety.

That person could use your address. He could find your house. Then he might bother you. That would be scary.

Tell an adult if a stranger asks for your address. He will not be angry. He will be glad you did the right thing. He will help you.

Never share your address online. Keep it private. This keeps you safe. That is why sharing your address is an Internet don't.

WORDS TO KNOW

Internet (IN-ter-net) A network that connects computers around the world. The Internet provides facts and information.

junk mail (JUNK MAYL) Mail that a person did not ask for and does not want.

private (PRY-vit) Not meant for strangers to know.

website (WEB-syt) A place on the Internet.

INDEX

WEBSITES

Due to the changing nature of Internet links, PowerKids Press has developed an online list of websites related to the subject of this book. This site is updated regularly. Please use this link to access the list:
www.powerkidslinks.com/idd/add/